Amazing Questions & Answers

Human Body

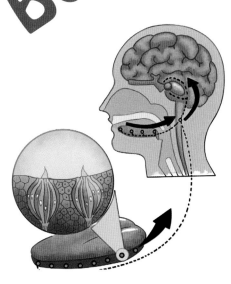

Om KiDZ
An imprint of Om Books International

First Published in 2019 by

Om KIDZ | Om Books International

Corporate & Editorial Office
A-12, Sector 64, Noida 201 301
Uttar Pradesh, India
Phone: +91 120 477 4100
Email: editorial@ombooks.com
Website: www.ombooksinternational.com

Sales Office
107, Ansari Road, Darya Ganj
New Delhi 110 002, India
Phone: +91 11 4000 9000
Email: sales@ombooks.com
Website: www.ombooks.com

How?

How do muscles work?

What?

Why do I have ears?

What makes my lips pink?

Why?

When?

When do I get infections?

CONTENTS

How does hair grow?

Your hair begins growing from a root on your head. The root is made up of protein. Blood from your scalp nourishes the root, and makes the hair grow. The hair then gets pushed up through the skin on your scalp as it grows.

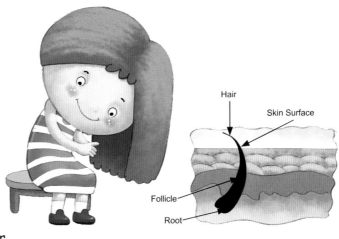

Hair

Skin Surface

Follicle

Root

Find out

How long can your hair grow in a day?

Pocket fact

I can support weight!
A single hair strand can hold about 100 grams in weight and an entire head of hair could bear up to 12 tonnes—the equal of two African elephants.

How do people go bald?

Everyone loses hair. Even you! In fact, you lose around 50 to 100 hair strands every day. As you lose hair, your body grows more to replace the ones you lost. But when someone goes bald, the body either stops producing new hair or it doesn't grow enough to replace all the lost ones.

How do different people have different eye colour?

Due to melanin in the iris! The colour of your eyes is due to the variations in the amount of melanin found in the front part of the eye, called the iris. When there is no melanin a person has blue eyes. A little melanin makes the eyes green. More melanin gives brown eyes and lots of melanin make eyes black.

Pocket fact

We usually blink about 2 to 50 times per minute. This adds up to about 10,000 blinks a day!

Try this

Have you ever tried to go from bright light to a dark room? What happens?

How do onions make me cry?

Onions make you cry when they are cut. When you cut onions, acidic chemicals are released. These chemicals react with the water in your eyes to form an acid called sulfuric acid. The sulfuric acid stings, making your eyes release tears to wash the irritant away.

How am I able to speak?

Thank your vocal cords! Vocal cords are flaps of tissues connected to a tube in your throat. By using the muscles in your throat, you can vibrate these vocal cords. When you do so, the air inside them also vibrates and makes a noise. This noise is what we hear when we speak or sing.

Vocal Cords

Find out

Some people have a very strong sense of smell. What is this called?

Pocket fact

Our ways are separate!
Your throat has the epiglottis, a flail which divides the food pipe from the wind pipe and protects the body from choking on food that could obstruct the airway.

How do I get a sore throat?

It's because of a virus! A sore throat refers to the pain, itchiness and irritation of the throat. It is triggered by a viral infection. Infections such as cold and flu are caused by viruses. When you get a sore throat, you may also have a runny nose, cough, hoarseness and red eyes.

> **How do hands become clean when I wash them with soap?**

They get rid of germs! When you wash your hands with soap, all the dirt particles and germs stick to the soap. The water then washes them away. This prevents the germs from spreading, and you from falling sick.

Pocket fact

I have the biggest hands! Lui Hua of China is the man with the biggest hands in the world. His left thumb is 10.2 inches long and his index finger is 12 inches long.

How fast do my fingernails grow?

Not so fast! Fingernails grow very slow. On an average, fingernails can grow about one tenth of an inch every month. If you lose most of a fingernail, it could take six months or more for it to grow back completely.

Find out

Do your nails sweat?

How do my feet stink sometimes?

Your feet have over 25,000 sweat glands which is a rich food supply for bacteria. When you cover your feet with socks, you make a perfectly dark and moist home for them. The bacteria that feed on your sweat leave behind their excreta after their meal and that's why your feet sometimes stink.

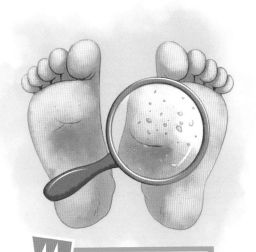

Pocket fact

I have the longest legs! Svetlana Pankratova from Russia is the woman with the longest legs in the world. They are 132 cm long!

Find out

How many bones are there in your feet?

How is athlete's foot caused?

Athlete's foot is a skin infection that is caused by a fungus. When infected, your feet gets bumps on them. The skin between your toes gets cracked and blistered. There is redness and scaling on the soles of your feet. The skin between the toes may look "cheesy" and have an unpleasant odour.

How do muscles work?

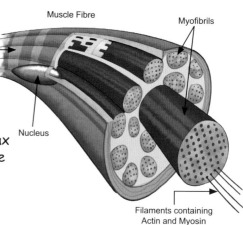

Muscle Fibre

Striations

Myofibrils

Nucleus

Filaments containing Actin and Myosin

Muscles are made of fibres. Fibres are long thin cells which are packed in bundles. These fibres contract and relax to makes the muscles work. Muscles are also attached to your bones, and help move the different parts of your body.

Find out

Some muscles like those of your heart and lungs are out of your control. What are such muscles called?

Pocket fact

Tetanus is dangerous!
Tetanus (or lockjaw) is a serious infection in muscles caused by bacteria that affects the brain and nervous system. It causes stiffness in the jaw and other muscles.

How do I get a sprain?

Your bones meet at joints that help your body move and bend. Strong, elastic bands of tissue hold bones together at the joints. A sprain happens when these bands have been overstretched or torn. Ankles, wrists, and knees sprain most easily.

How many times does my heart beat in a day?

On an average, the heart of an adult beats 72 times in a minute. The heart of a child beats between 90 to 120 times a minute. Hence in a day, an adult's heart beats 103,680 times and that of a child beats between 129,600 to 172,800 times.

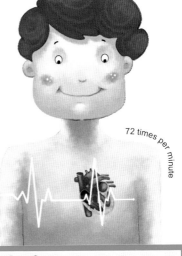

72 times per minute

Try this

Put a sea shell to your ear and listen to the noise it makes.

Pocket fact

I travel fast!
It takes just six seconds for blood to travel from the heart to the lungs and back. It takes eight seconds for it to travel to the brain and back, and just 16 seconds for it to arrive at the toes and travel all the way back to the heart.

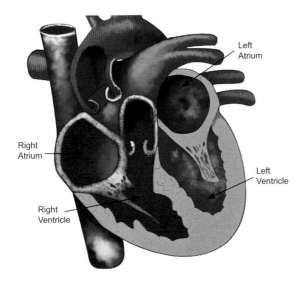

Left Atrium

Right Atrium

Left Ventricle

Right Ventricle

How many chambers are there in my heart?

Four! Your heart has two upper and two lower chambers. The upper chambers are called atrium. These receive blood from the body. The lower chambers are called ventricles. These pump blood out of your heart.

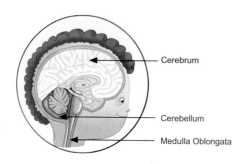

Cerebrum

Cerebellum

Medulla Oblongata

How big is my brain?

Your brain is as big as both your fists put together. The brain is the control centre of the body. It helps you think, feel, remember and a lot more! It also controls your inner organs and helps your body function.

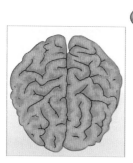

Pocket fact

Doctors can know about the working of your brain with the help of an EEG machine. It shows the electricity as waves on a screen and tells us how the brain works.

Find out

Can you name the three main parts of the brain?

How do I remember things?

Your brain helps you do so! Different parts of your brain do different jobs. One part helps you see, another part helps you think. A part of your brain known as cerebrum helps you remember things.

How are my bones held together?

By joints and strong bands! Your body has ligaments—a tough band of tissue that hold the ends of bones together at a joint. Joints are places where two or more bones meet. If your body did not have ligaments, your bones would be unable to work together!

Pocket fact

We are strong!
Human bones are four times stronger than concrete. A cubic inch of bone can bear a weight of 19,000 lbs.

Find out

How many bones does your hand have?

How does a doctor treat a fracture?

A cast helps the broken bone! Casts are made of bandages soaked in Plaster of Paris which hardens into a tough shell on drying. A doctor treats the fracture by putting on a cast to keep the bone in place for the few weeks it takes for the broken bone to mend.

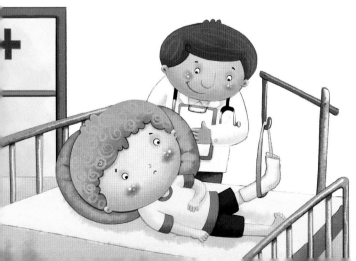

How does the doctor look inside my body?

Using special pictures called—X-rays! An X-ray is a picture of the inside of your body. An X-ray machine is used to take these pictures. A doctor can see broken bones, lung infections, cancerous growths with its help.

Try this

Put a stethoscope over your heart and count the number of times your heart beats in a minute.

Pocket fact

Before X-ray machines were invented, broken bones were diagnosed by physical examination and a doctor's best guess. On 8 November 1895, a German physics professor Wilhelm Conrad Roentgen discovered X-rays.

How can I listen to my heart beat?

Using a stethoscope! Usually you can't hear your heart beat, but with a stethoscope they get a whole lot louder! With it, you can hear your heart beat, the air going in and out of your lungs, tummy gurgles, and other noises that tell the doctor how things are working inside your body.

How do I get fever?

You have a fever when your body temperature rises above the 98.4 °Fahrenheit. Once germs enter your body, your brain gives a signal to raise the body temperature. Getting a fever is your body's way of fighting the germs and making the body a less comfortable place for them!

Try this

Using a thermometer, check the temperature of water at room temperature and then again when you take it out of the refrigerator. Compare the difference!

Pocket fact

It's not you!
Your immune system recognises the cells that do not belong to your body and attacks them. This happens when, for example, germs enter your body, they are destroyed by your immune system.

How does medicine know where I have pain?

Medicines don't directly go to the place where you are hurt. They work with your nerves and your brain to keep you from feeling the pain. When you take a medicine, it prevents injured cells from releasing chemicals. So, when the cells don't release chemicals, the brain doesn't get the signal to feel the pain. And your pain goes away!

How do I get allergies?

Allergy is your body's reaction to certain things that are usually harmless to most people. You get allergies when your body mistakenly believes that some substance is harmful to it and responds differently.You can be allergic to certain foods, dust particles, pollens or even medicines! Sneezing, itchy rashes, stuffy nose and diarrhea are some of the reactions to allergies.

ACHOO

Pocket fact

Hay fever!
The most common allergic disease that is caused due to pollens is the Hay fever. It causes sneezing, swollen eyelids and itchy eyes.

Find out

You use sanitizers, isn't it? How do they work?

How do germs enter my body?

In many ways! When you hurt yourself they can enter even through that small wound. If you touch something that may have germs and then touch your mouth or nose without washing your hands, they can easily enter your body.

How do we gain weight?

Your body keeps a track of what you eat and how much energy you burn. If you eat properly and exercise regularly, you don't have to worry. But if you overeat and do not exercise, the body stores all the extra food in the form of fat and you gain weight!

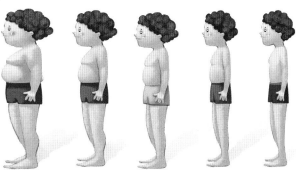

Pocket fact

A new lining!
You form a new stomach lining every three to four days. If that does not happen, then the strong acids used by your stomach to digest food would also digest the stomach.

Find out
Why do we need to exercise?

How do people age?

As we grow, our bodies go through many changes. Since we can't keep growing forever, eventually our bodies get old. People get old when their skin becomes loose and gets wrinkles, hair turns grey and bones begin to shrink.

What makes my fingerprints special?

Press your finger onto an inkpad and then to a piece of paper. You will see a print of the lines and ridges on your finger—that's your fingerprint. Each fingerprint is unique. This means that no one else in the world has the exact same set of lines that you have on your fingers. Not even identical twins!

Pocket fact

You need 34 muscles to move your fingers and thumb: 17 on the palm and 18 on the forearm.

Find out

Why do we have wrinkles on the back of our fingers?

What makes my foot go to sleep?

Blame your nerves for this! When you sit on your foot, you temporarily compress the nerves. These nerves are then unable to send messages back to the brain normally, and so for the moment you don't feel anything. It's as if your brain is saying "Hello", but your foot does not reply.

What makes me feel dizzy when I spin?

Your inner ears have fluid inside them. When you spin around, the fluid inside the ears moves too. Even when you stop, the fluid continues to move for a while, bends tiny hair and sends a signal to your brain. This makes you feel like you are spinning backward. We call that "feeling dizzy".

Pocket fact

Your ear has three bones. These are so small that they can be placed together on a penny. They are the stapes, malleus and incus.

Find out

Why is ear wax important?

What does my outer ear do?

Your outer ear is called the pinna or auricle. The outer ear's job is to collect sounds and channel them through the ear canal towards the middle ear so that you can hear various sounds.

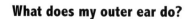

What makes my nose run?

There is a sticky substance in your nose called mucus. Your nose runs when you catch a cold or flu. This mucus keeps the germs out of your lungs and the rest of the body.

Pocket fact

A 12-year-old girl from UK, Donna Griffiths, holds the world record for the longest sneezing bout. She began sneezing on 13 January 1981 and kept sneezing for 978 days!

Find out

Some people have a very strong sense of smell. What is this called?

What makes me cough?

You cough because of excess mucus or when you inhale irritants that are present in the air. These irritants lie on the surface of your respiratory tract and the body tries to push them out in the form of cough. Coughing helps to clear the throat.

What does my tongue do when I sleep?

Your tongue never rests even after talking, swallowing, tasting and germ-fighting all day long. When you fall asleep, your tongue is busy pushing saliva into the throat to be swallowed. If it doesn't do that, you would be drooling all over your pillows!

Find out

How many taste buds does a human tongue have?

Pocket fact

The tongue is the only muscle in your body that works without any support from the skeleton. This is known as muscular hydrostat.

What helps my tongue taste food?

The taste buds on your tongue let you know if the things you eat are sweet, salty, sour or bitter. Taste buds have tiny bumps (papillae) and sensitive, microscopic hair called microvilli. These hair send messages to the brain about how something tastes.

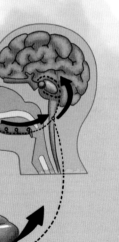

Microvilli

Papillae

What is cavity?

A cavity is a hole in the tooth caused due to decay or breakdown of the tooth. You get cavities because of a sticky substance (plaque) that carries germs. The bacteria in your mouth make acids and when plaque clings to your teeth, the acids corrode the tooth enamel.

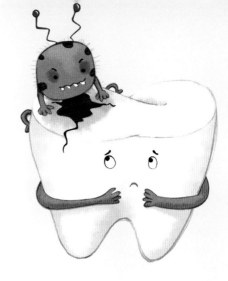

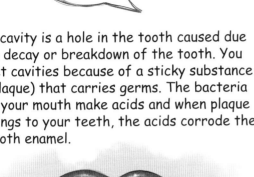

 Pocket fact

Oh I have Odontalgia! The scientific term used to describe toothache is 'Odontalgia'.

What makes my lips pink?

The skin on your lips has only three to six layers of cells compared to the 16 layers of skin covering other parts of the body. This makes the skin on your lip almost transparent. Your lips appear red or pink because of the blood capillaries that lie under this transparent surface of your lips.

Find out
Can your lips sweat?

What helps my eyes see different colours?

Your eyes have small cones that sense colour. Cones sense shades of red, green, or blue colour. Together, these cones can sense combinations of light that enable our eyes to see millions of colours.

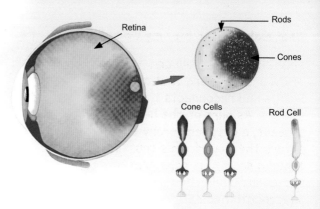

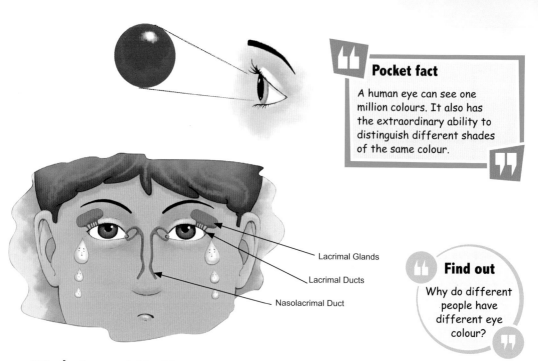

Pocket fact

A human eye can see one million colours. It also has the extraordinary ability to distinguish different shades of the same colour.

Lacrimal Glands

Lacrimal Ducts

Nasolacrimal Duct

Find out

Why do different people have different eye colour?

What's the special bathing system for my eyes?

Tears bathe your eyes! There are special glands called lacrimal glands, above the outer corner of each eye where tears are produced. Every time you blink, tears come out of the upper eyelid. Tears help to wash away germs, dust and other particles that can harm your eyes. Tears also keep your eyes from getting dry.

What makes scabs over my wound?

Your skin makes collagen—a tough, white protein fibre that acts like a bridge and reconnects the broken tissues. As part of the healing process, a dry, temporary crust covers the wound. This crust is called a scab. The scab protects the wound while the damaged skin underneath heals.

Pocket fact

Deep down in your skin, there are touch receptors called Ruffini Endings. They are sensitive to being stretched or squeezed, and they also respond to changes in temperature.

Find out

Where is the thinnest layer of skin on your body?

What gives me goosebumps?

When you feel cold or are scared, your body releases a chemical called adrenalin. This causes the little muscles at the base of each hair to contract and stand up. When this happens, your body creates an insulating layer and keeps your body warm. Goosebumps are just your body's way to make sure that you keep warm in the cold weather!

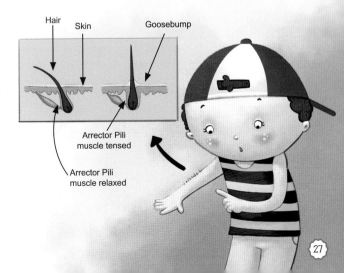

Hair   Skin   Goosebump

Arrector Pili muscle tensed

Arrector Pili muscle relaxed

What is the strongest muscle in my body?

It twists, turns, bends and helps you talk! It's your tongue! When it comes to doing different kinds of work, your tongue is probably the strongest muscle in your body. It is made up of many groups of muscles that run in different directions to carry out all the tasks—talk, swallow or taste.

Pocket fact

Muscles get most of their energy from glucose. Glucose is made from carbohydrates such as sucrose (from sugar), lactose (from milk) or fructose (from fruits).

Find out

There are different types of muscles in your body. But what are heart muscles called?

What makes my muscles cramp?

Your muscles cramp when they lock up, and you feel pain. This happens when one or more of your muscles contract and do not relax again (this is called a spasm). Exercising for too long, sweating and not drinking enough water can lead to a muscle cramp.

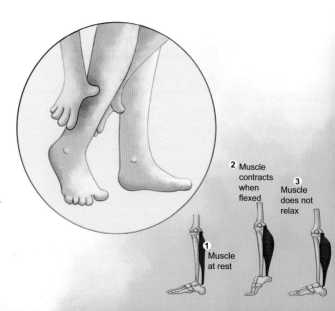

2 Muscle contracts when flexed

3 Muscle does not relax

1 Muscle at rest

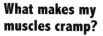

What are my bones made of?

Bones are made up of calcium, blood vessels and marrow. Around 70 percent of the bones in your body are made of calcium. The bone is hard, smooth and solid outside, and porous and spongy inside. A bone also has room for blood vessels which makes our bones slightly bendable. At the centre of bones is a softer substance called the marrow.

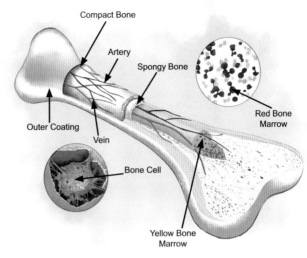

Compact Bone

Artery

Spongy Bone

Red Bone Marrow

Outer Coating

Vein

Bone Cell

Yellow Bone Marrow

Find out

How many bones does a baby have? What happens to the bones as it grows?

Pocket fact

In the olden days, whale bones were used to make corsets for women and men. These corsets would squash in a person's body so that he or she looked slimmer.

What makes my joints pop?

The popping bubbles in your joints make that sound! The joints on your body are where the bones meet. A thick liquid called synovial fluid surrounds your joints to keep them lubricated. Sometimes gases are pushed in the synovial fluid. When you stretch your joints far enough, gas bubbles pop and produce the popping sound that you hear.

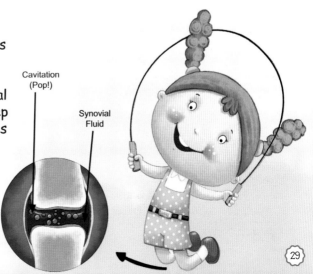

Cavitation (Pop!)

Synovial Fluid

What is inside my brain?

Your brain contains millions of nerve cells. These cells are grey, white and pink (a few of them) in colour and have texture like tofu! They are connected end-to-end and come together to make up the brain, vertebral column and the nervous system.

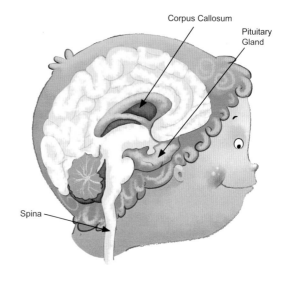

Corpus Callosum

Pituitary Gland

Spina

Find out

Have you heard about ice cream headaches? Why do we get them?

Pocket fact

The cerebrum (largest part of the brain) is divided into two halves. The left half controls the right side of the body and the right half controls the left side.

What is a headache?

Headache is not actually caused by pain in your brain. In reality, your brain can only tell you when other parts of your body hurt but can't actually feel pain. Sometimes the muscles or blood vessels that cover your head swell and become larger, causing pain. The surrounding nerves immediately send a rush of messages to your brain, and that is when you get a headache.

What do I have a belly button for?

Your belly button is the spot where your umbilical cord was once attached. The umbilical cord carries oxygen and nutrients from the mother to the foetus inside the womb. But once a baby is born, it doesn't need an umbilical cord. The doctor cuts the cord and a tiny stump is left. When this stump falls off after a few weeks, you are left with a belly button.

Find out

How long does it take for food to reach your stomach?

Pocket fact

Acid in the stomach!
Your stomach contains hydrochloric acid which helps in digestion and kills bacteria and viruses that may enter the body along with the food you eat.

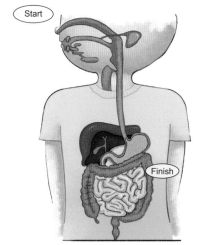

Start

Finish

What happens when food goes inside my body?

The food you eat gets digested. Food is broken down into simple substances (such as glucose or glycerine) in your body. This process is known as digestion. Digestion takes place in two different parts: the stomach and small intestine. Your stomach releases juices and churns food. These juices turn large food particles into smaller ones, which are absorbed in the blood.

What is locked inside my rib cage?

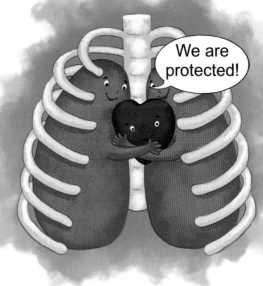

We are protected!

Your heart and lungs are the important organs that the rib cage protects. Lungs help you in respiration and the heart pumps blood into your body. Your ribs act as bodyguards, protecting your heart and lungs. If you didn't have ribs, these organs would be in danger every time you walk down the street or play sports!

Find out

What is a stethoscope used for?

Pocket fact

Your heart pumps about 100 gallons of blood through the body each hour—enough to fill 1,600 drinking glasses.

What makes my heart go 'lub-dub'?

The 'lub-dub' of your heart is the sound of your heart beat! Your heart does the important job of pumping blood and oxygen throughout the body. There are tubes that carry blood and oxygen around your body from the heart. The sound of your heart beat is made by these tubes as they open and close to pump blood in and out.

What are tonsils and tonsillitis?

Tonsils are lumps of soft tissue located at the back of your throat on both sides. They help fight infections. Tonsillitis happens when your tonsils become infected by bacteria or viruses. Your tonsils may become red and swollen, or have a white or yellow coating on them.

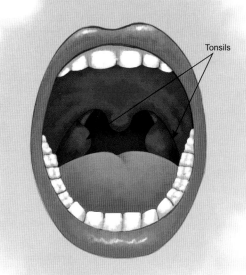

Tonsils

Find out

The pharynx at the back of your nose and mouth carries both air and food. Then why doesn't food enter your windpipe?

Pocket fact

Ear! Nose! Throat!
A doctor who takes care of all these parts is called an otolaryngologist.

What is the Adam's apple?

It's another name for your voice box or larynx. Your larynx grows larger in your teens and sticks out from your throat. This is called the Adam's apple. Everyone's larynx grows during their teens, but larynx in girls doesn't grow as much as it does in boys. That's why only boys have Adam's apple!

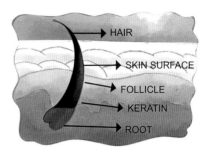

HAIR
SKIN SURFACE
FOLLICLE
KERATIN
ROOT

Why do I have hair on my head?

You don't have hair only on your head. In fact, your whole body is covered in millions of tiny hair that you can hardly see! Hair contains a hard material called keratin, which is made up of dead cells of a tough protein. The hair on your head keeps it warm and cushions your skull.

Find out

Hair grows almost everywhere on your body. Can you discover which parts of your body don't have any hair?

Pocket fact

Why do old people have grey hair?
Hair is black, red or blonde because it contains a lot of melanin. As people grow older, melanin in the hair gets reduced and it turns grey, silver or white.

Why doesn't it hurt when the barber cuts my hair?

The parts of your hair that lie above the skin's surface are made up of dead cells and there is no sensitivity or nerve sensation—unlike the other parts of the body—in them. Thus, when the barber cuts your hair it doesn't hurt.

Why can't I see anything in the dark?

When light falls on objects that are lying in front of you, it enters your eyes and passes through the iris and pupil to reach the lens. This is how you see objects. The lens focuses these rays onto the retina forming an image that your brain interprets. In the dark, there's no light that can reflect the object. This means there is no signal sent to your brain and this is why we can't see anything.

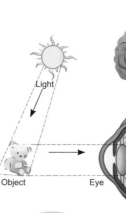

Brain

Light

Object   Eye

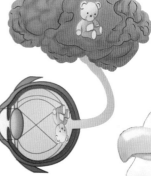

Find out

Look into the mirror. There's a space between your eyebrows. What is this space called?

Pocket fact

Animal senses are stronger than or very different from ours. An eagle can see things from more than 3 times as far as we can.

Why do I blink?

Oil producing glands are located under your eyes. When you blink, these glands lubricate the eyes and provide moisture that prevents your eyes from drying. Blinking also prevents dust particles from entering and irritating your eyes.

Why do I have a nose?

Your nose allows you to smell various scents! This is a big reason why you can taste things. The nose is the main gate to your respiratory mechanism—body's system for breathing. The nose has two openings called nostrils that let the air into your body.

Try this

Eat something holding an onion under your nose. What do you observe?

Pocket fact

Your sneeze can travel at about 100 miles per hour!

Why do some people snore?

People snore when they can't breathe freely through their nose and mouth while sleeping. It is often caused by the narrowing of the airway, either due to poor sleep posture or abnormalities of soft tissue in your throat.

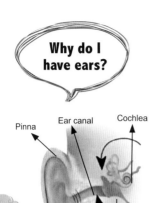

Why do I have ears?

Pinna
Ear canal
Cochlea
Ear drum

Ears help you hear different sounds. There are tiny bones inside the ear that help a sound move into the cochlea—a small, curled tube in the inner ear. The cochlea is filled with liquid and lined with tiny hair. When sound enters into the liquid, it applies pressure on the tiny hair. This triggers a signal to the brain, and you hear sounds.

Pocket fact

Your sense of balance depends on the vestibular system located in your inner ear. The moment you close your eyes, your ears cannot correlate and you will lose balance.

Try this

How many sounds can you recognise? Blindfold your friend and produce different sounds by clapping, jingling coins in a jar. Now, ask your friend to guess the sound.

Why do my ears 'pop' inside an airplane?

Due to air pressure! As the plane goes up, the air pressure decreases, but the air pressure in your ear is the same as what it was when you were on the ground. The air pressure inside your ears is more than the air pressure in the airplane. The air in the ear then presses against the ear drum and you feel as if your ear drums will burst.

Why do I sweat when I cycle?

To cool you down! Your body works best when its temperature is about 37 °Celsius (98.6 °Fahrenheit). When you run or exercise, you sweat. Sweating is your body's way of cooling you down. Moisture from sweat glands under the skin comes out in the form of sweat. As the sweat dries, your body cools down.

Pocket fact

When you touch something hot, nerves quickly send a message to the brain or spinal cord, which immediately commands the muscles to take your hand away. All this happens in a split second.

Find out

Which part of your body has the thickest and the thinnest skin?

Why does my skin get tanned if I spend a lot of time in the sun?

The colour of your skin is due to a pigment called melanin. Melanin prevents your skin from getting damaged under the sun's rays. When you go out into the sun, the skin begins to produce more melanin to protect itself from the sun's ultraviolet (UV) rays. Over a long period of time, this melanin accumulates under your skin and gives you a tan.

Why does my mouth water when I smell delicious food?

Your mouth and nose are closely linked. When you smell something yummy, your mouth wants to have it. Your body gets ready to eat by producing saliva. That's why your mouth waters when you smell something delicious.

Try this

- Collect some food items.
- Use a clean paper towel to dry your tongue.
- Taste each food, one by one. How does it taste?
- Have some water.
- Taste each food item again and let your saliva do the magic!

Pocket fact

Can you swallow your tongue?
The tongue is firmly connected to the bottom of your mouth by a membrane called frenulum. So you can never swallow your tongue even if you try!

Why do we burp?

When you eat or drink quickly, you swallow air along with your food. But your body does not need this air. This air comes back the same way it went down your throat and you burp.

Why do my milk teeth fall when I grow up?

You usually start losing your milk teeth between the age of 6 and 7. Your milk teeth fall because, as a baby, your jaws are too small to hold permanent teeth. Once you grow up, the root of your teeth become loose. The weakened milk teeth then fall out and the permanent teeth push through the gums.

Pocket fact

The white covering of your teeth is known as the enamel. Enamel is a tough, shiny substance and it acts as the tooth's personal bodyguard. Enamel works as a barrier, protecting the inside parts of the tooth.

Find out

Why do some people wear braces?

Why do my teeth chatter when it is cold?

To keep you warm! The part of the brain called the hypothalamus keeps your body at a constant temperature of 37 °Celsius (98.6 °Fahrenheit). When it's cold outside, the brain sends a message to your body that it needs to warm up. The chattering of your teeth is just another form of shivering.

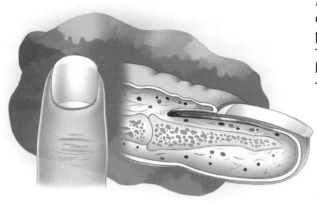

Why do I have fingernails?

A nail is a protective covering on the tip of your finger. It protects your fingertips and the skin below. Fingernails also help us feel things and pick up tiny objects.

Find out

Why are the tops of your nails white and the rest pink?

Pocket fact

Tinea is a fungal disease that can affect toenails. It is often called athlete's foot and is an itchy red rash between the toes with white, soggy-looking patches of skin peeling off.

Why do my fingers and toes wrinkle when left in the bathtub?

Your skin is covered with a special oil called the sebum, which lubricates and makes your skin waterproof. Staying in water for a long time washes away the sebum, allowing water into your skin's surface and your skin becomes waterlogged and contracts. This causes wrinkles on your fingers and toes.

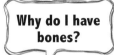

Why do I have bones?

Bones give shape and support to your body. If you didn't have bones, you would be like jellyfish! Bones make up the framework of your body called the skeleton. Without your backbone and leg bones, you wouldn't be able to stand up straight. Bones also protect the softer inner organs of your body. For example, the skull is like a helmet which protects your brain.

Pocket fact

Have you ever hit your elbow and felt a tingling sensation? That's because you have hit your 'funny bone'! It doesn't really hurt, does it? The 'funny bone' got its nickname because of that strange sensation you get after you hit it.

Why do my knees bend?

The place where two bones meet is called a joint. Some joints move and others don't. Your knees have hinge joints that are movable. These joints are like the hinges on a door. Just as most doors can only open one way, you can only bend your arms and legs in one direction.

Try this

Can you work out which joints are hinge joints? Just move your body around and the answers will be easy to find!

Why do I have a brain?

Your brain is very important. Without it, your heart wouldn't pump, and you wouldn't breathe. Your ears wouldn't hear and your fingers wouldn't feel or even move! Brain is the control centre for your body. It gives commands to various parts of your body, and makes it work.

Find out

Your heart is the size of your fist. But how big is your brain?

Pocket fact

Your brain is very soft. The bones of the skull protect your brain.

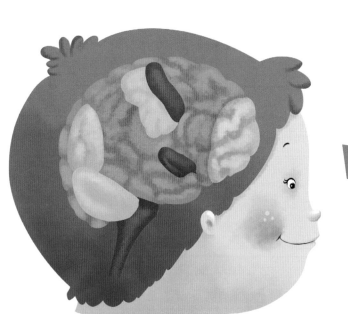

Why do I fall asleep?

After having worked for long hours during the day, you start feeling tired. This is your brain's way of telling you that it needs rest. You need to sleep because your body needs time to repair. Your mind needs to rest and relax while you are sleeping.

Why is blood red?

One of the main things that make up blood is red blood cells. These special cells contain a pigment called haemoglobin. Haemoglobin contains iron and carries oxygen throughout the body. Haemoglobin reacts with oxygen and gives your blood a bright red colour!

Find out

How many times does your heart beat in a day and a year?

Pocket fact

Your blood has white blood cells that protect you against germs or foreign bodies. There are around 5,000 to 7,000 white cells in a millilitre of blood!

Why does a cut stop bleeding after some time?

When you get a cut that bleeds, some special cells in your blood called platelets rush to the site of the injury. They attach with each other and stop the blood from flowing out. Calcium, certain vitamins and protein also join together with the platelets to cover the wound. The wound then heals in a few days.

Why do I feel thirsty?

The thirsty feeling you experience is your body's way of letting you know that you need to replace the water your body has lost while exercising or playing. When your body loses water, there is less saliva which causes your mouth and throat to feel dry.

Pocket fact

Obesity happens when there is an imbalance between how much you eat and how much energy you burn off. That's why we shouldn't eat too much fatty food.

HIC   HIC

HIC

Find out

Why does sour food make your lips pucker?

Why do I get hiccups?

There is a large muscle under your lungs called the diaphragm. It helps your lungs expand and contract. Sometimes when you eat too fast or swallow air, your diaphragm contracts too quickly. The air rushes into your lungs at a much quicker pace than usual. This rush of air then hits your voice box, causing hiccups!

There are many things that can make you sick. There is a group of tiny invaders called germs that can make your body sick. Do you know that germs are afraid of soap and water? If you wash your hands and body well, you can beat these tiny monsters.

Why do I fall sick?

Find out

Why does the doctor use a stethoscope when you are ill?

Pocket fact

Drinking milk is the easiest way to get the calcium you need. You would need to eat $2\frac{1}{2}$ cups of broccoli just to get the same amount of calcium that a cup of milk contains.

Why does the doctor give me injection?

An injection with liquid vaccine keeps you from getting some serious diseases such as tetanus and polio, among others. Vaccinations are given through an injection with a needle. A syringe holds the liquid vaccine, and the needle has a hole in it to squirt the liquid.

When do I need to wear spectacles?

When you have trouble seeing clearly! Everyone's eyes are a little different— the way they work and how well they see. Sometimes all the parts of the eye do not work the way they should. So, we wear spectacles that help us see more clearly.

Pocket fact

The eyes of famous scientist Albert Einstein are still preserved in a safe box in New York City even after 60 years of his death!

Healthy Eye

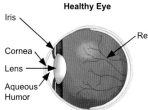

Iris
Retina
Cornea
Lens
Aqueous Humor

Infected Eye

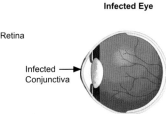

Infected Conjunctiva

Try this

Look at the picture and identify which line is longer.

Eyes play tricks too! The lines are actually equal in length!

When do I know I have conjunctivitis?

If the conjunctiva (the lining of the eyelids and the white of the eye) gets sore, red and watery. Mostly it is caused by a viral or bacterial infection. It can also be caused by allergies, hay fever, chlorine from swimming in pool water and sometimes it is a side effect of illness like measles.

When were my first teeth visible?

Your teeth were not visible from the day you were born. Although you had the beginnings of your first teeth even before you were born, they were not visible until you were about 6 to 12 months old. After your first tooth broke through, more and more teeth began to appear!

Pocket fact

The first toothbrush was invented in the year 1770 by William Addis in England!

Find out

Why do teeth have different shapes?

When does the dentist remove wisdom teeth?

If they do not grow in properly! The dentist usually removes wisdom teeth when the jaw is not large enough to fit all the teeth that are growing in and the mouth becomes overcrowded. He also removes them when these teeth are either stuck in your jaw or develop a cyst.

When does my breath smell?

If there are odour producing bacteria in your mouth! Bacteria accumulate on the food particles stuck between your teeth when you don't brush properly and floss regularly. The sulfur compounds released by these bacteria make your breath smell!

Find out

What is voice mimicry?

Pocket fact

The first toothpaste ever made was a mixture of wine and pumice! It was made almost 5,000 years ago in Egypt.

When does my voice begin to change?

It's a different timetable for everyone! Some voices might start to change earlier and some might start a little late. Generally, your voice will begin to change between the ages of 11 and 15. When you reach this age, your body begins making hormones which cause the larynx to grow and vocal cords to get longer and thicker. This changes your voice. Both boys and girls experience voice changes as they grow older, but a boy's voice may change more than that of a girl.

When do I get infections?

When germs enter your body! You have billions of germs inside and on the outside of your body. Many of these germs help you keep healthy in many ways. Infections are caused by germs which do not belong in your body. Your body may be affected by bacterial, viral, fungal and parasitical infections.

Find out

Can you name the first natural antibiotic? Who discovered it?

Pocket fact

In 2013, a bacteria was found in New Zealand that is unaffected by every single antibiotic known!

When do I need to take antibiotics?

If under a bacterial attack! Antibiotics are types of medicines that will find and kill bacteria in your body that make you sick. You need to take antibiotics in conditions such as pneumonia or acne. Antibiotics can work very well against bacteria, but they don't work against viral diseases such as cold, flu or ringworm.

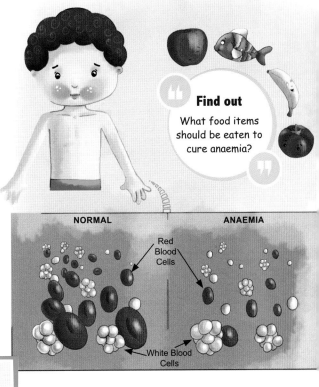

When does my body become anaemic?

If there is a lack of iron! When you are not getting enough iron in your diet you develop a deficiency. This means that your body cannot make haemoglobin, so it makes fewer red blood cells. When you are anaemic, less oxygen reaches the cells and tissues, which affects the working of your body.

Find out

What food items should be eaten to cure anaemia?

NORMAL | ANAEMIA

Red Blood Cells

White Blood Cells

Pocket fact

Your body has enough iron in it to make a three-inch long iron nail!

When does a heart murmur occur?

A heart murmur is a whooshing sound between your heart beats. The whoosh is a noise that the blood makes as it flows through the heart. An abnormal heart murmur can develop if the heart has a hole, a leak in the valve, or if the valve doesn't open all the way.

Aortic Valve Open

Ruptured Aortic Valve Closed

When does a cut need stitches?

Stitches are for cuts and wounds that a doctor believes may not heal correctly on their own. To heal completely and correctly, the sides of a cut must be close to each other, so that the skin can grow back together. It takes 4 to 14 days for the cut to heal and your stitches to be removed.

Pocket fact

Many years ago spider web was used for dressing wounds. Doctors did this to stop the bleeding!

Find out

What are the symptoms of tetanus?

When do I need a tetanus shot?

Tetanus is a disease caused by bacteria. You usually get a series of four tetanus shots before turning 2 years of age, followed by a booster dose at 4 to 6 years of age. If you get a dirty or deep wound then the doctor may suggest another tetanus shot just to be on the safe side!

When does my body steal calcium?

If you do not have enough calcium in the body! Your bones store minerals for when the body needs them. If you don't consume enough calcium in food, your body steals it from your bones. So, to keep your bones healthy, drink plenty of milk.

Pocket fact

A human and giraffe both have 7 bones in their neck – the bones in giraffe's neck are just a bit longer!

Find out

Have you heard about a greenstick fracture? What is it?

When do I need a cast?

If you ever break a bone! You will need a cast to hold the pieces of a broken bone steady while they are healing. Casts are wrapped around the broken bone and can be made out of plaster of Paris, fibreglass or plastic and even air, which is called an air cast.

When do pimples occur?

Your skin has oil glands that make sebum to lubricate your hair and skin. As the body begins to mature and develop, these oil glands generate more sebum. Then the pores of our skin open, allowing sebum, bacteria and dead skin cells to make their way under the skin—and you're left with a small, red bump called a pimple!

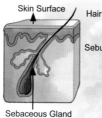
Skin Surface

Hair
Sebum
Sebaceous Gland

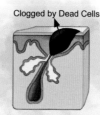
Clogged by Dead Cells
Sebum Buildup

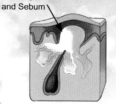
Infection, Pus and Sebum

Pimple

Pocket fact

Our skin cells are being replaced all of the time. We lose 30,000-40,000 cells every minute—that's over 43 million skin cells every day!

Find out

What can you do to prevent sunburns?

When do I get scalds?

When you get burnt by hot gases or liquids! A scald is a burn caused by hot water, steam or other liquids like coffee or tea being spilled from a mug, or the water from the hot water tap in the bath. Touching hot utensils with hot liquid in it can also cause scalds. Many times people have been scalded by spaghetti Bolognese!

When are germs good for me?

When they are the harmless kind! Some good bacteria live in your intestines and help you use the nutrients in the food you eat and make waste from what's left over. Some bacteria are also used by scientists in labs to produce medicines and vaccines!

Try this!
Unscramble the letters of the word given below. It is the name of bacteria. Do you know where it lives?

E. olic

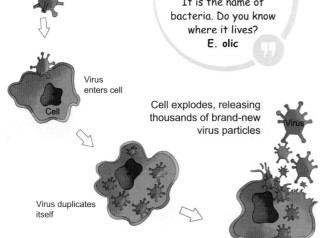

Virus

Virus enters cell

Cell

Cell explodes, releasing thousands of brand-new virus particles

Virus

Virus duplicates itself

When are viruses active?

When inside a living cell! Viruses are microorganisms that need to be inside living cells to grow and reproduce. This living cell is called the host. When viruses enter your body, they can spread and make you sick. Viruses cause chickenpox, measles, flu and many other diseases.

When do I feel thirsty?

When the water levels in your body gets low, it lets you know by making your feel thirsty. There are thirst receptors in the back of your throat that dry up when there's less water in your body. These receptors send a message to your brain telling it that you are thirsty and need to drink water.

Find out

What will happen if you don't have a stomach?

Pocket fact

Despite being called so, your small intestine is actually four times as long as the average adult's height. If it weren't looped back and forth upon itself it wouldn't fit inside the abdominal cavity!

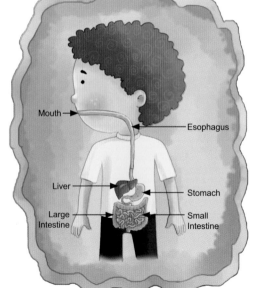

Mouth

Esophagus

Liver

Stomach

Large Intestine

Small Intestine

When does food get digested completely?

It varies from person to person! After you eat, it takes about 4 to 12 hours for food to get digested completely. Food from your mouth reaches the stomach and passes to the small intestine. It then enters your large intestine for further digestion and, finally, elimination of undigested food.

When are my muscles out of control?

Involuntary muscles are out of your control and work on their own. For example, the muscles in your heart, which keep blood pumping around your body, the muscles in your digestive system which move food down to your stomach all work constantly and are not in your control.

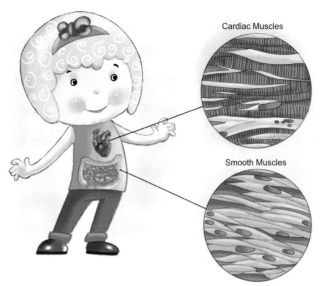

Cardiac Muscles

Smooth Muscles

Find out

Where do your muscles get energy from?

Pocket fact

You use 200 muscles to take one step. That's a lot of work for the muscles considering most of us take about 10,000 steps a day.

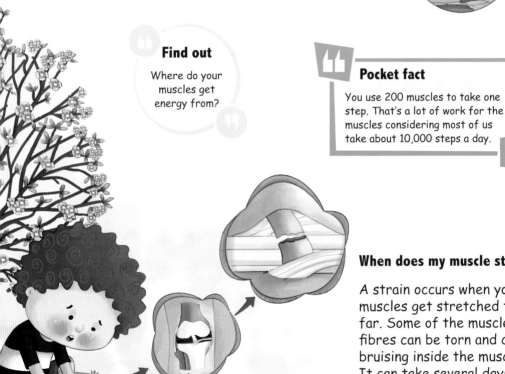

When does my muscle strain?

A strain occurs when your muscles get stretched too far. Some of the muscle fibres can be torn and cause bruising inside the muscle. It can take several days for the fibres to heal and for the bruising to go away!

When is my brain the most active?

At night! When you turn off, your brain turns on. After your body's day long work, it's the brain that works at night when you have fallen asleep. It makes you feel relaxed and works with the healing process of your body.

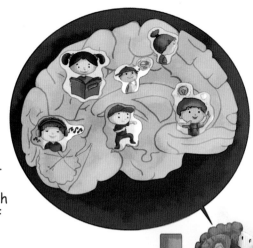

Find out

How long does the brain keep growing?

Pocket fact

Brain Bank!
Harvard maintains a Brain Bank where over 7,000 human brains are stored for research purposes.

When do I get a migraine?

A migraine is a painful headache that may occur with vomiting and numbness. It begins when blood vessels in the brain temporarily contract, causing the quantity of blood and oxygen flowing to the brain to drop. This, in turn, causes other blood vessels to expand. These blood vessels become inflamed and cause a migraine. Migraines can occur about one to four times a month. The pain is often throbbing and can happen on one or both sides of the head.

When do men start growing a moustache?

Between the age of 11 to 21 years! The first facial hair starts growing at the corners of the upper lip between 11 to 15 years of age. It then spreads to form a moustache over the entire upper lip between 16 to 17 years of age. However, in some men moustaches grow fully by the age of 21 years.

Pocket fact

The longest moustache!
Ram Singh Chauhan of India has the longest moustache. From end to end, it is 4.2 metres, or 14 feet in length. He has been growing the moustache for 44 years, and regularly massages it with oils, and washes it.

Find out

Who was the oldest living person on earth?

When will I stop growing?

Not until you are in your late teens! Both boys and girls will have a growth spurt and grow to their adult height between 13 to 19 years of age. A few boys may grow taller even into their early twenties!

Index

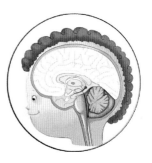

OTHER TITLES IN THIS SERIES

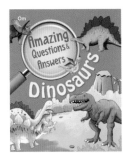

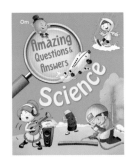